AF270618

Gorgons

by Grace Hansen

Abdo Kids Jumbo is an Imprint of Abdo Kids
abdobooks.com

abdobooks.com

Published by Abdo Kids, a division of ABDO, P.O. Box 398166, Minneapolis, Minnesota 55439.
Copyright © 2024 by Abdo Consulting Group, Inc. International copyrights reserved in all countries.
No part of this book may be reproduced in any form without written permission from the publisher.
Abdo Kids Jumbo™ is a trademark and logo of Abdo Kids.

Printed in the United States of America, North Mankato, Minnesota.

102023

012024

THIS BOOK CONTAINS
RECYCLED MATERIALS

Photo Credits: Alamy, Depositphotos Enterprise, Getty Images, Granger Collection, Shutterstock

Production Contributors: Teddy Borth, Jennie Forsberg, Grace Hansen
Design Contributors: Candice Keimig, Pakou Moua

Library of Congress Control Number: 2023937689
Publisher's Cataloging-in-Publication Data

Names: Hansen, Grace, author.

Title: Gorgons / by Grace Hansen

Description: Minneapolis, Minnesota : Abdo Kids, 2024 | Series: World of mythical beings | Includes online
    resources and index.

Identifiers: ISBN 9781098268596 (lib. bdg.) | ISBN 9781098269296 (ebook) | ISBN 9781098269647
    (Read-to-Me ebook)

Subjects: LCSH I. Gorgons (Greek mythology) Juvenile literature. | Mythical animals Juvenile literature. |
    Folklore--Juvenile literature. | Legends--Juvenile literature.

Classification: DDC 398.2454--dc23

Table of Contents

The Myth of the Gorgon 4

Homer & Hesiod 6

Looks & Lore 12

Then & Now 20

More Creatures of Greek
Mythology 22

Glossary 23

Index 24

Abdo Kids Code 24

The Myth of the Gorgon

Gorgons are mythological creatures. "Gorgon" comes from the ancient Greek word *gorgós*. It means "**grim**" or "terrible."

Homer & Hesiod

The ancient Greeks heard frightening stories about gorgons. A single gorgon was described by the Greek poet Homer. This monster lived in the **underworld**.

Later, the Greek poet Hesiod described three gorgons. Their names were Stheno, Euryale, and Medusa. They were the daughters of the god Phorcys and goddess Ceto.

ARCHITEKTVR PLAS

In Hesiod's stories, Medusa was **mortal**. Her sisters were immortal. They would live forever.

Looks & Lore

Some stories describe Medusa as very beautiful. Others said she had hideous tusks, fangs, and a forked tongue.

Many stories agree that the goddess Athena became angry with Medusa. She turned Medusa's hair into snakes. Anyone who looked at Medusa would turn into stone.

The most famous story about
Medusa involves her death.
The Greek hero Perseus was
tasked to take her head.

BENVEN[VTVS] [CE]LLI[N]I

When Perseus cut off Medusa's head, two creatures came from her. One was Pegasus, a winged horse. The other was **Chrysaor**.

19

Then & Now

Greek soldiers brought Medusa with them to battle. They put Medusa's face on their helmets and shields to protect them from their enemies. Today, Medusa can be seen in ancient Greek art.

More Creatures of Greek Mythology!

Glossary

Chrysaor – the son of Medusa and Poseidon and the brother of Pegasus. Chysaor is sometimes described as a giant or a winged boar.

grim – horrible or frightening in a serious way.

mortal – not living forever.

underworld – in Greek mythology, a distinct realm where an individual goes after death.

Index

appearance 12, 14

art 20

Athena 14

Ceto 8

Chrysaor 18

Euryale 8, 10

Greece 4, 6, 20

Greek mythology 4, 6, 8, 10, 12, 14, 16, 18

hair 14

Hesiod 8, 10

Homer 6

Medusa 8, 10, 12, 14, 16, 18, 20

Pegasus 18

Perseus 16, 18

Phorcys 8

Stheno 8, 10

Visit **abdokids.com** to access crafts, games, videos, and more!